JAN 0 6 2017

ELK GROVE VILLAGE PUBLIC LIBRARY

3 1250 01168 3442

Discarded By Elk Grove
Village Public Library

P9-BZP-100

ELK GROVE VILLAGE PUBLIC LIBRARY
1001 WELLINGTON AVE.
ELK GROVE VILLAGE, IL 60007
(847) 439-0447

MILITARY
CAREERS

Careers in the US Coast Guard

Toney Allman

ReferencePoint
Press®

© 2016 ReferencePoint Press, Inc.
Printed in the United States

For more information, contact:
ReferencePoint Press, Inc.
PO Box 27779
San Diego, CA 92198
www.ReferencePointPress.com

ALL RIGHTS RESERVED.
No part of this work covered by the copyright hereon may be reproduced or used in any form or by any means—graphic, electronic, or mechanical, including photocopying, recording, taping, web distribution, or information storage retrieval systems—without the written permission of the publisher.

Picture Credits:
Cover: US Coast Guard/Petty Officer Jonathan R. Cilley
  6: Accurate Art, Inc
10: US Coast Guard/Petty Officer 2nd Class Annie R.B. Elis
18: US Coast Guard/PA1 Adam Eggers
44: US Coast Guard/Petty Officer 2nd Class Etta Smith
54: US Coast Guard/PA2 Mariana O'Leary

LIBRARY OF CONGRESS CATALOGING-IN-PUBLICATION DATA

Allman, Toney.
  Careers in the US Coast Guard / by Toney Allman.
    pages cm. -- (Military careers)
  Includes bibliographical references and index.
  ISBN 978-1-60152-936-7 (hardback) -- ISBN 1-60152-936-8 (hardback) 1. United States. Coast Guard--Vocational guidance. I. Title.
  VG53.A525   2016
  363.28'602373--dc23
                                                                            2015034212

Contents

The Unique Military Service

The US Coast Guard is the smallest of the five military branches, but it is the oldest lifesaving organization in the world. The other military branches stress combat, but while it may become involved in combat missions, the Coast Guard stresses protection, rescue, and law enforcement on the nation's waterways, along the coastlines, and at sea. The Coast Guard is a multi-mission maritime military force tasked with three basic roles: safety, security, and stewardship. As explained in the 2011 Department of Homeland Security white paper on the US Coast Guard, safety, security, and stewardship mean simply that the Coast Guard's job is to

- Protect those on the sea;
- Protect the nation from threats delivered by sea; and
- Protect the sea itself.

Multiple Missions

The Coast Guard's main responsibilities are subdivided into eleven official missions. The three safety missions are search and rescue (for anyone in trouble in the nation's waters); marine safety (promoting safe boating practices; investigating maritime accidents; and inspecting merchant vessels, oil rigs, and port facilities); and aids to navigation (mapping the waters and maintaining buoys, lighthouses, and markers). Security includes four missions. They are illegal drug interdiction (stopping drug smuggling); undocumented migrant interdiction (enforcing immigration laws at sea and returning illegal migrants safely to their home countries); port, waterway, and coastal security (mainly counterterrorism preparedness and response); and defense readiness (military preparation for any threats to ports, harbors, and coastlines). Finally, the four missions involving stewardship are marine environmental protection (protecting the ocean ecosystem and preventing water pollution); living marine resources (maintaining and protecting marine species); ice operations (conducting icebreaking operations in the Great Lakes, the polar regions, and the extreme Northeast); and other law enforcement (including preventing illegal international fishing in the exclusive economic zone extending 200 nautical miles from all US coastlines).

These eleven missions mean that the Coast Guard operates along more than 100,000 miles of US coastlines and inland waterways and safeguards 3.4 million square nautical miles of ocean. With such great responsibility, it is little wonder that the Coast Guard's motto is *Semper Paratus*, or "Always Ready." It is a huge job, but the Coast Guard has always risen to the challenge.

Before it was known by its modern name, the Coast Guard began its mission as the Revenue Cutter Service in 1790. Established by the first secretary of the treasury, Alexander Hamilton, its major responsibility was to collect customs duties and tariffs from merchant ships at the new nation's ports of entry. In 1915, by an act of Congress, the service was merged with the US Life-Saving Service (which had been established in 1848) to form the Coast Guard. In 1946, Congress transferred the Bureau of Marine Inspection and Navigation to the Coast Guard as well. Although the Coast Guard began its life under the authority of the Treasury Department, today it is under the Department of Homeland Security. During times of war, it can be transferred to the Department of Defense, which has happened twice in Coast Guard history—in 1917, during World War I; and in 1941, during World War II.

Joining the Coast Guard

With only about 38,000 active members (not counting reservists and auxiliary members), today's Coast Guard is a highly selective military service. In the military as a whole, about 20 percent of applicants are accepted, but in the Coast Guard, less than 4 percent of applicants are accepted for enlisted service. The acceptance rate for people applying

US Armed Forces: Pay

In the US Armed Forces, pay for both enlisted personnel and officers depends on rank and years of service. Promotions depend on performance in addition to number of years served, with higher ranks translating to higher pay grades. The two graphs show monthly salaries commonly reached in the first four years of service.

Enlisted Pay

Monthly Salary Ranges for Enlisted Personnel with 0–4 Years in Service

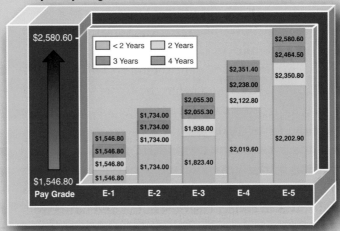

Officer Pay

Monthly Salary Ranges for Officers with 0–4 Years in Service

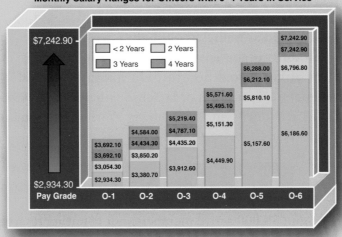

Note: Monthly salary ranges in both graphs are based on enlisted and officer pay scales effective January 1, 2015. The pay scales described here do not take into account the value of health benefits or housing and other allowances.

Source: Defense Finance and Accounting Service, "Military Pay Charts, 1949 to 2015," December 23, 2014. www.dfas.mil/militarymembers/payentitlements/military-pay-charts.html.

to the US Coast Guard Academy to become officers is about 16 percent. Whether as an enlisted member or an officer, getting into the Coast Guard is not easy, but many applicants seek to serve. In the book *Rescue Warriors: The U.S. Coast Guard, America's Forgotten Heroes* by David Helvarg, then-eighteen-year-old enlisted recruit Amber Nethercutt explains, for example, "It's the hardest service to qualify for, and I like the fact that we don't kill people, we save people."

No matter which path members take, each must meet physical and educational requirements, be a citizen or permanent resident, be between seventeen and twenty-seven years old, and pass a background check. Enlisted recruits must have a high school diploma. They are also required to pass the Armed Services Vocational Aptitude Battery (ASVAB) with a satisfactory score. The ASVAB is an aptitude test that measures skills and ability in such areas as arithmetic reasoning, word knowledge, paragraph comprehension, and mathematical knowledge. It also measures aptitudes for different career paths. Once accepted, recruits then must go through eight weeks of basic training, during which they are challenged mentally and physically. Each recruit must also pass a final swim test.

Officer applicants must take and pass the ASVAB, SAT, or ACT with a satisfactory score to qualify. Officer candidates must have college degrees or be working toward a four-year degree to apply to Officer Candidate School (OCS). Otherwise, candidates may apply to the Coast Guard Academy, which is a four-year college program. Qualified enlisted personnel may also apply for OCS. Some 60 percent of the candidates attending OCS are enlisted personnel, moving up in the ranks. OCS is a seventeen-week program that is similar to basic training except that it also includes coursework in navigation, leadership, management, and seamanship. These skills are taught at the Coast Guard Academy as well.

Abounding Opportunities

No matter what path a Coast Guard member takes, job opportunities and opportunities for advancement in ranks—called "rates" for enlisted personnel—are many and varied. Every job in the Coast Guard is available to both men and women, on land, at sea, or in the air.

Members may serve at sea on cutters, which are the large vessels more than 65 feet (19.8 m) in length with living quarters. They may serve on a variety of boats (under 65 feet), such as motor lifeboats and law enforcement craft. Jobs on cutters and boats include seamen, firemen, mess cooks, mechanics, electricians, navigators, gunnery mates, and information technicians, among others. The Coast Guard also fields aircraft; jobs in the air arm include aviation mechanics and electricians; survival technicians, such as rescue swimmers and emergency medical technicians (EMTs); aviators and helicopter pilots; and many more. On land, members may hold jobs in marine science, public affairs, health services, engineering, or as commanders of sectors or districts covering large areas of the United States or in the USCG Headquarters in Washington, DC.

Coast Guard members have careers on both sea and land, depending on assignment. Skills in high demand for enlisted personnel and officers include math, science, engineering, and computer science. Operations specialists and food-service specialists are sought after, as well as doctors, nurses, and lawyers. There is a job for almost every skill in the Coast Guard, and all "Coasties," as they proudly refer to themselves, are committed to saving lives and protecting the coastlines and waterways of America.

Boatswain's Mate

What Does a Boatswain's Mate Do?

A boatswain's mate (BM) is a master of seamanship and one of the most versatile members of the Coast Guard's team. BMs are the sailors who can perform almost any job involving deck maintenance on boats and ships, supervising the seamen on deck, navigating, and performing small boat operations. They serve on every vessel in the Coast Guard fleet, as well as at duty stations on shore. In general, a boatswain's mate can load cargo, stand watch duty, perform navigation, set gangplanks, and handle the ropes, cables, lines, hoists, chains, and winches used on any vessel. The website USMilitary.com says that the boatswain's mate "is a jack-of-all-trades when it comes to shipboard operations."

BMs have to be skilled and knowledgeable in everything they do on deck. Even handling hoists, cables, and chains is not easy. For example, each spring, the Coast Guard buoy tender *Katherine Walker* swaps out and inspects about 300 winter buoys marking navigation channels in the Hudson River and other New York waterways. The win-

At A Glance:
Boatswain's Mate

Minimum Educational Requirements
High school diploma

Personal Qualities
Physically fit; adaptable to the seagoing experience

Certification and Licensing
First aid and CPR certification; twelve-minute swim test

Working Conditions
On board vessels or at shore stations

Salary Range
Monthly salary depends on pay grade and years of service

Number of Jobs
Approximately 4,800

Future Job Outlook
Stable

Boatswain's mates from the US Coast Guard cutter Stratton *take part in training in the Pacific Ocean. Among the most versatile members of the Coast Guard, boatswain's mates are skilled in navigation and boat handling, deck machinery, and seamanship.*

ter buoys are relatively small, steel, torpedo-shaped markers that are not likely to be damaged or moved by winter ice. But the summer buoys are large, 26-foot (8-m) steel markers equipped with solar-powered lights and radar sensors. They are crucial to the safety of commercial and recreational boats that navigate New York's waterways from spring through fall. Replacing winter buoys with 7,800-pound (3,500-kg) spring buoys is a dangerous, physically demanding job. Deck workers, supervised by boatswain's mates, use cranes and cables to haul the winter markers out of the water, get them on deck, and then push them across the deck to be stowed away properly.

Next, the large summer buoys have to be attached to mooring chains, hauled from the deck, and placed in the correct position in the water. The chains are so heavy that workers have to use sledge hammers and big steel hooks to maneuver them around the deck. The work can be perilous because a chain that slips as the buoy is swaying across the deck could snap and do terrible injury to the seamen. Experienced Boatswain's Mate Troy Krotz supervises his team with an eye to the difficulties. In a 2015 *New York Times* article, he explains to reporter Corey Kilgannon, "You're dealing with quite a big amount of weight that at any moment could become quite violent, so you have to make sure you're not between the load and a hard point. When that live chain starts running and you're between 10,000 pounds of concrete and steel, you'll lose that fight every time." Still, one by one, every spring, Krotz ensures that the buoys are replaced without incident.

On many small boats, such as tugs, rescue lifeboats, and patrol boats, BMs function as officers in charge. They drive the boats and often perform as federal law enforcement officers. This means conducting boat inspections and boarding civilian boats and ships to be sure that safety regulations and federal laws are being followed. One such BM describes some of his activities to Lt. Stephanie Young in the *Coast Guard Compass*, the official blog of the Coast Guard. He says, "My name is Logan Kellogg, and I am a third class boatswain's mate at Coast Guard Station Seattle, Wash. . . . Our primary missions at Station Seattle include: search and rescue, escorting Washington State Ferries, cruise ships and U.S. Navy vessels, as well as conducting an average of 600 vessel boardings each year."

How Do You Become a Boatswain's Mate?

Education

BMs are enlisted service members. In preparation for this career, the Coast Guard recommends that high school students take algebra, geometry, and shop classes.

Once an enlisted member has completed basic training and a required four-month first assignment, he or she can apply to BM "A" School (Class A, or basic school). The school is fourteen weeks of intensive training and instruction. Students receive classroom and practical instruction in navigation and running the school's small boats. They learn marlinespike seamanship, which is the practical knowledge of lines, ropes, knots, and cordage used on any vessel. They receive leadership training and learn first aid and CPR. In addition, students undergo intensive physical training. In a 2010 article about Boatswain's Mate "A" School in the *Coast Guard Compass*, the school chief, Senior Chief Petty Officer Todd Stein, explains, "The physical fitness standards help [students] manage and mitigate the mental and physical rigors of long work hours and intense operations during their careers."

Upon graduation from "A" School, the service member becomes a petty officer 3rd class, with a Coast Guard rate of E-4. In the Coast Guard, enlisted ranks are called rates, and the rates E-4 through E-6 are petty officer grades. Petty officers are the technical workforce of the Coast Guard. Throughout their careers, BMs have many opportunities to take on more responsibilities and training and advance through the petty officer rates.

Certification and Licensing

Boatswain's mates must get their first aid and CPR certification in "A" School. Otherwise, no other licensing or certification is required for this job, but all boat crew members in the Coast Guard must be able to pass a standardized twelve-minute swim test.

Volunteer Work and Internships

Although swimming skills are not required to join the Coast Guard, every recruit must learn to swim. Anyone interested in becoming a boatswain's mate will have a head start if he or she already demonstrates swimming ability. Volunteering or working as a lifeguard would be an advantage. The Coast Guard also suggests that any experience with small boats is very helpful. Young people interested in becoming BMs might work at a marina or participate with family members in activities such as piloting or repairing small boats.

Physical Requirements, Skills, and Personality

Boatswain's mates must have good hearing and normal color vision. They need to have leadership skills because they are often in charge of deck crews or the crews of small boats. Physical strength and a high level of manual dexterity are absolutely necessary. BMs must competently operate cranes, winches, hoist chains, and heavy ropes; stow cargo; tie a variety of knots; as well as run deck equipment. Math skills are critical to navigation.

At the online bulletin board Reddit, one BM describes the personality that makes the job of boatswain's mate perfect for him. Mikel Cartwright says he chose the Coast Guard for the adventure. He adds, "I became a boatswain's mate (bm) because driving fast boats is about the most fun you can have sober." Other BMs talk about desiring the genuine seagoing experience and enjoying hands-on action.

On the Job

Working Conditions

Some boatswain's mates serve on large cutters and may be at sea for months at a time. Boatswain's Mate Paul Vanacore, for example, served on the high endurance cutter *Sherman* on a tour around the world. In David Helvarg's 2009 book *Rescue Warriors: The U.S. Coast Guard, America's Forgotten Heroes*, Vanacore remembers,

> We left Alameda and went to Hawaii, Guam, Singapore, Japan, the Persian Gulf, the Seychelles, Madagascar, Cape Town [in] South Africa—where we helped rescue a car carrier that was dead in the water and listing badly in fifteen-foot swells—then on to Cape Verde, Barbados, Aruba, through the Panama Canal to San Diego and home, where we were greeted like returning heroes with roses dropping from the Golden Gate Bridge and a band waiting at the pier.

Other BMs operate out of shore stations and on many different kinds of boats. At Coast Guard Station New Orleans, for instance, boat crews patrol 7,500 square miles (19,425 sq km) of waterways, lakes, and swamps, enforcing federal laws and performing safety checks on recreational vessels. Such a job is not without its dangers because of the chance of drug smuggling and other criminal activities. Before they go out on patrol, boat crews suit up in body armor and carry flashlights, batons, pepper spray, handcuffs, and handguns. The members of the station also perform search-and-rescue missions when they get reports of missing vessels or boats in trouble.

In addition to buoy tenders and patrol boats, BMs may serve on icebreakers off the shores of Alaska or drive motorized lifeboats along the Outer Banks of North Carolina. They may work off the coast of Florida performing immigrant or drug interdiction. Working at sea, however, can place BMs in terrible danger. In 2012, Master Chief Boatswain's Mate Terrell Horne III was killed off the California coast when a drug smuggling vessel deliberately rammed his small Coast Guard boat. Other BMs have suffered injuries or died during perilous rescue missions. For a boatswain's mate, no day is guaranteed to be an ordinary day.

Earnings

Military pay is standardized and based on the member's enlisted rate and seniority. In addition to basic pay with automatic pay raises every one to two years, all enlisted members are eligible for supplemental payments and allowances, such as combat pay, flight pay, and food and housing allowances.

Opportunities for Advancement

With experience and further training, BMs may become chief petty officers, senior chief petty officers, and master chief petty officers with rates between E-7 and E-9. They may be leaders with command and supervisory positions and the drivers in charge of small boats. BM advanced training can be for specialties such as coxswain (small boat captain), heavy weather coxswain, or buoy deck supervisor, among other jobs. Heavy weather coxswains complete advanced "C" School training at the National Motor Lifeboat School, where they learn to captain rescue lifeboats in all sorts of bad weather conditions.

A select few BMs qualify to operate as surfmen. Currently, the Coast Guard has about 200 surfmen. They are the only coxswains qualified to operate in breaking waves. They are the skilled captains of motorized rescue lifeboats at the twenty coastal stations where treacherous surf is a problem. In 2013 Boatswain's Mate Victoria Taylor became only the sixth female ever to qualify as a surfman. In a *Coast Guard Compass* article written by Kelly Parker, Taylor says,

> Our forefathers intentionally rowed small wooden boats into storms and surf, wearing cork life jackets

and wool uniforms. It was cold, wet, physically demanding and dangerous. They didn't do it for the paltry wages; they did it to save lives. We're much better equipped to do our jobs now, but I think that many of us have a similar attitude today. We wait—some of us our whole careers—for that one good case where we can help someone get home to their families. I am proud and honored to have been accepted into the community, and hope that I can live up to their legacy.

What Is the Future Outlook for Boatswain's Mates?

Today, the Coast Guard has about 4,800 boatswain's mates. The Coast Guard is a highly selective military service and its retention rate is high, but according to the Bureau of Labor Statistics, opportunities for qualified individuals should remain good through 2022.

What Are Employment Prospects in the Civilian World?

Many BMs make the Coast Guard a career, but those who choose to return to civilian life may qualify for jobs such as pier superintendent, tugboat crewman, heavy equipment operator, marina supervisor, marina operator, and ship pilot.

Rescue Swimmer

Rescue swimmers are the renowned heroes of the Coast Guard who lower themselves by ropes or cables or jump from helicopters into the water in order to rescue people. Their job is one of the most dangerous in all the military. Formally known as aviation survival technicians (ASTs), these brave service members specialize in water rescue under any conditions. They may drop into rough, freezing seas to grab a stranded fisherman floating in a life vest after his boat sinks, land on the deck of a ship to retrieve a person with a medical emergency far from shore, save people from flooded homes or cars, or pluck people from cliffs and caves. The rescue swimmer reaches the person in trouble and gets him or her into a rescue basket that is lowered from the helicopter and then raised to safety. Then the rescue swimmer is hauled back into the helicopter where he or she is responsible for the emergency medical care of the victim until the helicopter reaches land. The creed of Coast Guard rescue swimmers is "So others may live," even at risk of their own lives.

Petty Officer Christopher Austin's first rescue out of one of the Coast Guard's twenty-four

At a Glance:
Rescue Swimmer

Minimum Educational Requirements
High school diploma

Personal Qualities
Mentally and physically fit; self-confident; good under pressure

Certification and Licensing
EMT certification; secret security clearance

Working Conditions
On helicopters out of air stations

Salary Range
Monthly salary depends on pay grade and years of service

Number of Jobs
About 300

Future Job Outlook
Stable

air stations where aircraft are based, exemplifies the job of the rescue swimmer. In 2010, his Astoria, Oregon, station received a call that a fishing boat had overturned in Willapa Bay, Washington, with two people on board. Austin's helicopter crew searched for about forty minutes until they spotted one man clinging to some crab pot buoys in thick fog and fighting heavy waves. Austin was lowered into the water on a rescue hook. In a 2012 interview for the *Coast Guard Compass*, he remembers,

> When I was lowered, he was literally going under the water's surface, so I grabbed him with a big 'ol bear hug, and took one of the worst beatings of my life in the surf. The waves were relentless, and I soon became the center of the rope in a tug of war between the helicopter and the ocean. That part wasn't fun. . . . His mouth was foaming, his eyes were glassed over and even his nose and his eyes were foaming out sea water. I thought he had already expired and my heart suddenly sank to the bottom of that bay faster than his ship had. . . . We pulled him all the way up and immediately began CPR.

Austin's emergency efforts were successful, and the man began breathing again. The other person on the boat was never found, but the fisherman Austin rescued not only survived but made a full recovery.

How Do You Become a Rescue Swimmer?

Education

Rescue swimmers are enlisted service members. Because aviation survival technicians are responsible for many different kinds of aviation equipment, the Coast Guard recommends that high school students take algebra and geometry in preparation for this career.

Once an enlisted member has completed basic training and a four-month wait in a first assignment, he or she can apply to be accepted into the Airman Program. This is a four-month-long training program at an air station. At the completion of the program and with the commanding officer's recommendation, the member may apply to AST "A" School to become an aviation survival technician. Before attending actual AST training, each candidate must complete a physical fitness training program of four to six weeks. The physical fitness standards are so high that only 50 percent of candidates make it through this first phase. AST School itself is also a rigorous, demanding course. It lasts eighteen weeks and is followed by three weeks of EMT training. On average, more than 50 percent of these "A" School

A US Coast Guard rescue swimmer practices a freefall deployment in the Gulf of Mexico. Specialists in all types of water rescues, rescue swimmers have pulled stranded fishermen and boaters from rough seas and plucked people from rooftops during floods.

attendees are also unable to complete the program, but those who fail may be allowed to try again at a later time.

Physically and emotionally, AST School is taxing and extremely stressful. It has to be. The goal of the program is to make the candidate comfortable and confident in heavy seas and dangerous situations. Each student must have the endurance, strength, and courage to function for thirty minutes under the worst rough sea conditions. Training includes a lot of classroom work; physical fitness tasks (such as swimming in an icy river and then running for 5 miles (8 km) in wet clothing); and instruction in high-tech, 12-foot-deep (3.7 m) swimming pools with wave machines, 15-foot (4.6 m) towers to jump from, and thunder, lightning, fog, rain, and wind machines. Trainees in the pools must demonstrate strong swimming ability under all these conditions. For example, a student may have to tread water for an hour while holding a 10-pound (4.5 kg) weight. He or she must be able to swim underwater for a minimum of 25 yards (22.8 m) without coming up for air, swim 500 yards (457 m) in twelve minutes, and tow a buddy while swimming for 200 yards (183 m). Then comes the brutal demand to successfully complete different rescue scenarios in the pools. In *SJ Magazine*, AST Caleb Flippen describes the challenge to writer Heather Morse in an article titled "So Others May Live." Flippen says, "Lots of collegiate swimmers and polo players who are great swimmers fail out of the program. You have to learn to think and carry out a rescue while submerged, holding your breath and getting tossed around by huge waves. You learn very quickly during training that if you panic, you will die while on the job."

One of the worst rescue tests that students must pass is called the "noncompliant survivor test." In this test, in simulated heavy seas in the pool, the student must leap into the water from a tower to simulate a helicopter drop. In the pool below is an instructor playing the role of drowning victim. As the student swims to the victim and tries to save him, the victim panics, flails around, hits and grabs onto the rescuer, and often pulls both student and victim beneath the waves. Very frequently, the would-be rescuer fails the test and only breaks free from the victim without saving him. Instructors offer no sympathy. In the magazine *Men's Journal*, a 2013 article written by Mathew Power titled "Inside the Coast Guard's Rescue Swimming

School" describes the demoralizing outcome of one noncompliant survivor test. Chief Petty Officer Ken Kiest was a lead instructor on the day Power observed. Kiest yelled at one student who failed to save his victim, "You let the survivor die; is that correct? Would you do that in the real world, let my daughter die? You fit to train? Are you fit to train?"

The mental challenges of training are designed to break down overconfidence while ensuring that the trainee can think clearly under pressure, act decisively, and never panic. After passing the noncompliant survivor test, students must face other more difficult tests, such as dealing with multiple victims in the water or rescuing a downed pilot still attached to a parachute. Because rescue swimmers may face even more difficult challenges in the real world of water rescue, they are pushed as hard as possible during training. Once they graduate, new rescue swimmers know that they have accomplished something few have ever done.

Certification and Licensing

Rescue swimmers must pass the National Registry of Emergency Medical Technicians (MREMT) examination so that they can provide prehospital care to rescued victims. All ASTs also must pass a background check and obtain a secret security clearance to ensure that the individual can be trusted with national security information.

Volunteer Work and Internships

Because strong swimming skills are critical for rescue swimmers, students considering this career should take the Red Cross Ocean Lifeguard course and experience working as a lifeguard. Increasing swimming strength by practicing different strokes and treading water every day might also be helpful, as would be joining a swim club.

Physical Requirements and Personality

Only people in superior physical shape are accepted into the AST program. Candidates must be able to pass a required air crew physical screening, have no orthopedic problems, and have normal color vision and normal hearing. Mental abilities must be high as well, as students must absorb a large amount of classroom information in a short time. Candidates are usually self-confident, very responsible, and good at focusing their attention on any task. In addition, successful candidates seem to have a large degree of emotional self-control, maintain calm under pressure, and feel a strong commitment to the job. Some psychologists suggest that successful rescue swimmers are "type A" personalities—competitive, self-critical, and goal-driven.

On the Job

Working Conditions

Rescue swimmers are members of helicopter flight crews, and they are assigned to every Coast Guard air station in the United States and Puerto Rico. At their air stations, rescue swimmers are ready for anything at any time, including flying training missions, inspecting and fixing all water lifesaving gear, and responding to SAR (search and rescue) cases. A typical work schedule might include six or seven twenty-four-hour on-duty shifts each month. While on duty, the rescue swimmer is prepared to suit up, grab gear, and get on board a helicopter within seconds of receiving an SAR call. He or she is always mentally ready to leap into action in extreme situations.

Earnings

Military pay is standardized and based on the member's enlisted rate and seniority. In addition to basic pay with automatic pay raises every one to two years, all enlisted members are eligible for supplemental payments and allowances, such as combat pay, flight pay, and food and housing allowances.

Opportunities for Advancement

ASTs may take advanced training in Advanced Helicopter Rescue School. This five-day program offers training in advanced techniques for heavy seas rescues, vertical rescues (such as off cliffs), and cave rescues. Training is also available in advanced EMT courses for becoming an operational fitness training instructor and to become a survival instructor at "A" School.

What Is the Future Outlook for Rescue Swimmers?

Acceptance for training is highly selective, and the retention rate for rescue swimmers is high. With only about 300 rescue swimmers in the Coast Guard, the chance of acceptance into and completion of the program is small. Yet the demand for qualified members, according to the Bureau of Labor Statistics, should remain good through 2022.

What Are Employment Prospects in the Civilian World?

Few rescue swimmers leave the Coast Guard for the civilian world. Those who do, however, may finds jobs as paramedics or EMTs, land and water survival instructors, commercial aircraft life-support equipment technicians, aircraft mechanics, aircraft ground handlers, and aviation maintenance instructors.

Electronics Technician

An electronics technician (ET) is responsible for all of the Coast Guard's electronic equipment, both on land and at sea. He or she manages, installs, repairs, and maintains equipment such as communications receivers and transmitters, navigation and search radar, electronic detection equipment, shipboard weapons controlled by electronics, command and control systems, and data and voice-encryption equipment. An ET, for example, can figure out which circuit board is responsible for a system failure, operate a weapons system by tracking and targeting the mark electronically, or stand watch in a cutter's radio room and monitor radar, watching for the blip signaling a fast small boat that might be carrying illegal drugs. When assigned to vessels, ETs may also be members of boarding teams. As a part of the vessel's law enforcement team, the ET may be helping to search boats and ships for smuggled drugs or enforcing maritime laws on foreign vessels in US waters.

Electronics technicians never know what problems they might

At A Glance:
Electronics Technician

Minimum Educational Requirements
High school diploma

Personal Qualities
Interest in electronics and computers; attention to detail

Certification and Licensing
CPR certification; security clearance

Working Conditions
On shore at stations and at sea on cutters

Salary Range
Monthly salary depends on pay grade and years of service

Number of Jobs
About 4,600 (including ETs, electrician's mates, and electrical technicians)

Future Job Outlook
Steady

be called upon to handle. In 2015, for example, a crew of ETs traveled to the Big Island of Hawaii in order to save the Coast Guard's Nationwide Differential GPS site from a threatened flow of lava from a volcanic eruption. This GPS system is critical to maritime operations and navigation around the state of Hawaii. The crew had to dismantle and move all this communications equipment before it could be destroyed by lava. The removal had to be done without damaging any equipment so that they could reinstall it when the lava danger had passed.

In a profile at the website Today'sMilitary.com, electronics technician Jennifer Foley explains her job:

> We're the ones who ensure that the ship and small boats can safely navigate and communicate with each other. We maintain most of the communications gear, like the VHF radios and the satellite communications. We also take care of the navigation and fire control radars, and the GPS. . . . On a mission, we are part of a task force. There are other cutters or Navy ships in the area and also your aircraft support—helicopters or fixed-wing planes—that you communicate with as well. We're also in touch with the unit that's in overall command of the area. A lot of times we'll have translators on board if we're going into another country's territorial waters. It can get a little hectic trying to keep track of everything.

Foley is proud of her contributions to the cutter on which she serves. She adds, "I'm not one of the people who goes out on the small boat and actually does the lifesaving or the rescuing. But I'm still part of an organization that goes out and that makes a difference in people's lives."

How Do You Become an Electronics Technician?

Education

Electronics technicians are enlisted service members. In preparation for this career, the Coast Guard suggests that high school courses such as physics, trigonometry, algebra, and shop are valuable. In addition, any education in radio or electricity is helpful.

Once a recruit has completed basic training, he or she is required to serve for a period of four months before applying to Electronics Technician "A" School for training. Basic electronics technician training at "A" School is one of the longest courses offered by the Coast Guard, taking twenty-eight weeks to complete. The school's curriculum begins with basic electricity fundamentals and safety, basic circuit analysis, basic electronic troubleshooting, and circuit analysis. It continues with courses in reading schematics, advanced circuit analysis, receivers, transceiver systems, VHF radios, radar, GPS systems, and operation of cryptographic equipment. Lab work includes soldering and utilizing all common coaxial and multiconductor cable connectors.

Upon graduation from "A" School, the service member becomes a petty officer 3rd class, with a Coast Guard rate of E-4. In the Coast Guard, enlisted ranks are called rates, and the rates E-4 through E-6 are petty officer grades. Petty officers are the technical workforce of the Coast Guard and are trusted with much responsibility as they acquire hands-on experience. The most important skill taught in "A" School, says Jennifer Foley, is the ability to function independently. She explains, "They gave us the tools that we need to go out in the fleet and figure out stuff on our own because, of course, nothing ever breaks the way it breaks in school."

Certification and Licensing

ETs are required to complete CPR certification. No other licensing is required for this job, but ETs must pass a governmental background check for a secret security clearance to ensure they can be trusted with national security information.

Volunteer Work and Internships

The Coast Guard says that any prior practical experience or work on any electronics systems is helpful for those wishing to become electronics technicians. Working as a hobby or more formally in telephone repair or with radios and transceivers could be a help in preparing for this career, as would computer maintenance and repair.

Physical Requirements, Skills, and Personality

ETs must have normal color vision and normal hearing. They need good attention to detail, above-average mathematical skills, and an interest in electronics and computer systems. Many ETs say that they enjoy the problem-solving part of their job. When something breaks down and they successfully repair it, they can feel like heroes! Also an ET is often called upon to climb masts and towers to maintain and test antennas aboard ships, so he or she cannot be afraid of heights or unable to climb and function with confidence. And because many ETs serve on vessels, a willingness to travel and be at sea for long periods is essential. Electronics technicians like the adventure, the travel, and the ever-changing demands of the job.

On the Job

Working Conditions

Electronics technicians are assigned to communications stations, to large cutters, and to all Coast Guard small and large shops at bases on shore. The large shops are called "electronics systems support detachments," and the small shops are known as "electronic systems support detachment details." From these shops where ETs are based, they are sent out to search-and-rescue stations and to any smaller cutters and boats to maintain and install electronic systems as necessary. Therefore, some ETs basically work on land, whereas others are at sea for long periods.

One ET on a cutter mentions an advantage of his working conditions: He points out that his work keeps him in the air-conditioned radio or radar room because the electronics equipment cannot be exposed to the heat. He also notes that most equipment functions well most of the time, so he is often not terribly busy. Another ET on a cutter emphasizes how things can go wrong in the corrosive sea air and in high-wind conditions. He is Petty Officer Jeremy Lyell, who can be seen repairing antennas atop a mast in a video on YouTube. Lyell explains that no one ever knows when something will break, but when it does, he must ensure that the more than 100 pieces of electronics equipment on board function correctly. Repairing a broken antenna that is critical to the vessel's communication systems is one of his jobs. He says, "It's a little nerve-wracking up there," but he competently works atop the mast in his harness, with his tools and gear hooked beside him, and replaces cables and cleans and weatherproofs connections.

Under different working conditions, Petty Officer Derek Severns's job is on land. He is assigned to the Coast Guard Communications Station New Orleans. A 2014 article in the *Coast Guard News* titled "Homerun Bound" reports, "Severns' job is to perform maintenance on a total of 15 transmitters, 17 receivers and 31 antennas that provide rapid, reliable and secure communications to the Coast Guard operational commanders, other governmental agencies and civilian organizations across the Gulf of Mexico." In the same article, Severns describes his job satisfaction. He says, "I was always intrigued with the opportunity to do something bigger than myself."

Earnings

Military pay is standardized and based on the member's enlisted rate and seniority. In addition to basic pay with automatic pay raises every one to two years, all enlisted members are eligible for supplemental payments and allowances, such as combat pay, flight pay, and food and housing allowances.

Opportunities for Advancement

With experience and further training, ETs may become chief petty officers, senior chief petty officers, and master chief petty officers with rates between E-7 and E-9. An electronics technician also may attend the Coast Guard's advanced training "C" School. Some may apply to "C" School directly after finishing "A" School; others may apply months or even years later. At "C" School, ETs acquire advanced skills in four major areas: communications, navigation, nationwide differential GPS, and IFF (identify friend or foe) systems. This is all computer-based technology, and "C" School graduates are able to maintain and troubleshoot in all technical areas of Coast Guard electronic equipment.

Some ETs are selected to attend the Coast Guard's Advanced Computer, Engineering, and Technology (ACET) program. This is a full-time, paid, two-year college program in which the service member can obtain an associate degree or a bachelor's degree in engineering or technology. Such graduates can receive officer commissions. Lieutenant Aaron Dahlen, for instance, was an electronics technician who attended the ACET program in 2004. Then for three years he served on icebreaker vessels in charge of electronics systems in a leadership position. In 2007 he received a commission as a lieutenant in the Coast Guard. After this, he decided to go to graduate school in the Coast Guard's Communications, Computer, and Electrical Engineering (CCEE) program and received a master's degree in electrical engineering. Then in 2012 Dahlen became a faculty member of the US Coast Guard Academy.

Lieutenant Dahlen achieved officer status through the Coast Guard's Direct Commission program, but other enlisted members choose to apply to the seventeen-week-long Officer Candidate School (OCS) and become ensigns upon graduation. After four years of service, any enlisted member with a rate of E-5 or higher and thirty college credits may apply to OCS. This is what now-Captain Lucinda Cunningham did. After graduating from college, she enlisted in the Coast Guard in 1990 and became an electronics technician. After four years of serving on a cutter, she applied to and was accepted at OCS. Eventually she attended graduate school and served as the executive officer at the Electronic Support Unit Boston. In 2015 she was promoted from commander to captain and assigned as the commanding officer of Coast Guard Base New Orleans. For those with the passion and motivation, there are no limits to the opportunities for advancement in the Coast Guard.

What Is the Future Outlook for Electronics Technicians?

According to the US Bureau of Labor Statistics, as of 2013 there were about 4,600 jobs in electronic and electrical equipment repair in the Coast Guard. The Coast Guard is a highly selective military service and its retention rate is high, but the Bureau of Labor Statistics predicts that opportunities for qualified individuals should remain good through 2022.

What Are Employment Prospects in the Civilian World?

Many ETs make the Coast Guard a career, but those who choose to return to civilian life may qualify for jobs such as an electronics technician, electronic installation technician, guidance systems specialist, data and satellite communication specialist, or in radio, television, or radar repair.

Aviator

What Does an Aviator Do?

The Coast Guard maintains more than 200 fixed-wing aircraft and helicopters. Aviators fly these aircraft on a variety of missions, but most of the Coast Guard's aircraft are helicopters. Helicopter pilots may operate off the flight decks of cutters or fly out of an air station on land. They may perform search-and-rescue missions, search for smugglers at sea, monitor fishing boundaries, or track oceanic oil spills. In fixed-wing aircraft—either propeller-driven or jet—pilots may find themselves flying law enforcement patrols, flying cargo planes, or conducting search-and-rescue or surveillance missions. Cargo planes may carry passengers, oil pollution control equipment, life rafts, or other equipment. Whatever their duties and whatever the aircraft, aviators in the Coast Guard must be able to fly in all kinds of weather conditions.

A good example of what Coast Guard aviators may be expected to do occurred during Hurricane Sandy on October 29, 2012. On that date, a replica wooden sailing ship, the *HMS Bounty*, was off the coast of North Carolina and trying to outrace the storm when it was hit by the fury of the hurricane's winds and raging seas. The ship

At A Glance:
Aviator

Minimum Educational Requirements
College degree; officer commission

Personal Qualities
Love of flying; mental stability and sharpness; leadership ability

Certification and Licensing
Aviator wings flight badge; certified on fixed-wing or rotary-wing aircraft

Working Conditions
Based at air stations and on cutters

Salary Range
Monthly salary depends on pay grade and years of service

Number of Jobs
Approximately 800

Future Job Outlook
Stable

lost power in its two diesel engines, began to take on water, and foundered. As the ship was sinking, it sent a rescue call out to the Coast Guard. Two of the sixteen crew members were washed overboard in their emergency immersion suits. Thirteen crew members made it to the two life rafts. The fate of the captain remains unknown.

Air Station Elizabeth City received and responded immediately to the call for help. First to arrive on scene was an HC-130J Hercules airplane—a long-range surveillance fixed-wing aircraft. Its pilot had to navigate through heavy turbulence with winds up to 60 knots (69 mph). The aircraft basically stood sentry, circling and keeping watch over the sinking ship and its survivors throughout the night and deploying flares to mark the position of the rescue operation.

Next, just at dawn, two rescue helicopters launched from the air station. The aviators were forced to fly at just 300 feet because of the storm conditions and had only an hour to rescue the people in the life rafts and return to the air station before running out of fuel. A drifting survivor was spotted and rescued first, and then each helicopter crew concentrated on a different life raft. As rescue swimmers plunged into the waters, got survivors into rescue baskets, and saw them winched aboard the helicopters, the pilots had to use all their skills to successfully recover all but the missing two of the sixteen crew members. All the time the pilots were hovering above the life rafts, the automated safety warning systems were repeating "altitude," "altitude," because they were too close to the giant waves. In an article titled "Shipmate of the Week–Rescuers of the HMS Bounty," posted by Lt. Stephanie Young for the *Coast Guard Compass*, copilot Jenny Fields describes the precision required of the pilots. She says, "The difficulty is not necessarily flying so low; but maintaining position with the liferaft and rescue swimmer in the water. The wind and waves were constantly pushing the targets through the water, so it was a lot of work for the pilots at the controls in the helicopters to stay in position."

Coast Guard aviators are highly trained in search-and-rescue missions. Liz Booker is a search-and-rescue helicopter pilot who described some of her experiences for the website *Girls with Wings*. She explains part of what her job entails, saying,

> As a qualified copilot, I moved to San Francisco, California, where I flew for 4 years and learned the arts of

hovering while hoisting baskets to small boats in the water, lowering the helicopter to within 15 feet of the ocean so the rescue swimmer could jump in to help people in trouble, and landing on the backs of ships. . . . Saving people who might die if we don't answer their call is tremendously rewarding.

How Do You Become an Aviator?

Education

Aviators are officers and must have a college degree. The Coast Guard offers several different paths to becoming an officer and an aviator.

High school students may apply for admission to the Coast Guard Academy in New London, Connecticut. It is a four-year college program that also prepares cadets to become junior officers—ensigns—upon graduation. Acceptance into the Coast Guard Academy can be difficult. Only about 20 percent of applicants are accepted every year. On average, successful candidates have SAT scores between 1750 and 2010 or ACT scores from 25 to 30. GPA ranges from 3.48 to 3.71 (out of 4). Approximately 250 young men and women are accepted into the academy each year. Graduates are required to serve a tour at sea before applying for flight school training to become an aviator. Flight school lasts eighteen to twenty-four months and covers academics, sea and land survival, and practical flight training, including helicopter, single engine, and multiengine fixed-wing aircraft. Officers can choose between helicopters and fixed-wing aircraft as a specialty.

Alternatively, those who are already college graduates, with a minimum GPA of 2.5 (out of 4), may apply to join the Coast Guard and attend Officer Candidate School (OCS). Enlisted members are also eligible to apply to OCS. To be eligible to become an officer, applicants must be US citizens and achieve security clearance. OCS is seventeen weeks of intense instruction in military lifestyle, leadership, physical training, navigation, ship's operations, and seamanship. Upon graduation, newly commissioned ensigns may apply to attend flight school and become aviators.

The Coast Guard also offers the College Student Pre-Commissioning Initiative (CSPI) for students at certain designated colleges and universities. This two-year scholarship program is open to sophomore and junior college students of high moral character and with high motivation to complete college who want to join the Coast Guard as officers. The students must be attending historically African American colleges and universities; Hispanic-serving institutions (in which a minimum of 25 percent of students are Hispanic); tribal colleges or universities; or the University of Guam, the University of Hawaii, Argosy University in Hawaii, or the Institute of American Indian and Alaska Native Culture. During their junior and senior years, students in CSPI spend about four hours a week in Coast Guard duties and undergo further training, such as basic training, during college breaks. When they graduate, the students are guaranteed a place in OCS. CSPI students can apply to the guaranteed flight program known as the Wilk's Flight Initiative (WiFI). Qualified students have to pass an aptitude test called the Aviation Selection Test Battery (ASTB) and pass a flight physical. At that point, they are guaranteed a position in flight school after graduating from Officer Candidate School.

Another pathway to becoming a Coast Guard officer and aviator is the Direct Commission program. Military pilots from other service branches who want to join the Coast Guard are eligible for this program. About 60 percent of Coast Guard aviators are direct commissions from other military branches.

Certification and Licensing

To be a pilot, a flight school attendee must earn his or her wings—the flight badge that certifies the graduate is a qualified aviator. In addition, all Coast Guard aviators must return to the Aviation Training Center for one week each year to maintain their training in their selected types of aircraft. An aviator is certified within the Coast Guard for either fixed-wing or rotary-wing (helicopter) piloting, depending on the flight school training completed. Usually new aviators are assigned duty as copilots and become first pilots after acquiring on-the-job flight experience.

How Hard Is It to Become an Aviator?

The Coast Guard aviation program is extremely selective. Approximately fifty applicants a year are chosen by the flight school selection panel to fill available flight training slots. Because the Coast Guard uses Air Force and Navy pilots who want to change services, only a few positions may be available for Coast Guard officers wanting to fly. For those officers, previous civilian flight training is not a consideration, but excellence in ability, supervisor recommendations, leadership, and aptitude examinations are absolutely necessary.

Physical Requirements, Skills, and Personality

The physical requirements for aviators are extensive and strict, and physical standards are high. Each applicant must pass both a flight physical and a physical fitness test. To be accepted for training, members must be between twenty-one and thirty-four years old and meet height and weight standards (because of such considerations as ejection seat limitations). Height must be between 62 inches (157 cm) and 77 inches (195 cm). There are also dental and vision requirements. A pilot must have no dental problems and no cavities, because tooth and gum problems may be affected by air pressure changes in flight. Eyesight must be 20/20 or correctable to 20/20 in both eyes, with uncorrected vision no worse than 20/50. Normal color vision, depth perception, and field of vision are also required.

All officers who become aviators are motivated and dedicated to a career as a pilot in the Coast Guard. They are able to be in command when piloting an aircraft and have mental sharpness and steadiness. Helicopter pilots have the self-confidence to fly in weather conditions in which other aircraft are grounded, and they have the trust in their own ability to accomplish instrument flying when visibility is poor. But most of all, pilots love to fly and consider their jobs the most exciting, challenging, and interesting in the world.

On the Job

Working Conditions

Pilots may be assigned to cutters, to air stations, or to a rescue station on the coasts. During a normal week they may fly three or four times, usually on two-hour training flights, but on rescue and patrol missions when needed. They stand duty and are on call for emergencies a couple times a month and also have desk time, when they complete paperwork, file reports, and perform administrative duties. A typical office day is from about 7:30 a.m. to 3:30 p.m., but irregular hours are common because of flight schedules.

Earnings

Military pay is standardized and based on the member's officer rank, time served, experience, and hours of flight time. In addition, officers receive housing and living allowances, medical and dental coverage, paid vacation, life insurance, and medical benefits.

Opportunities for Advancement

Along with rescue swimmers and other air crew members, helicopter pilots may attend Advanced Helicopter Rescue School, where they learn to function under high-sea and heavy weather conditions.

Advancement in rank comes with flight hours and years of service—from copilot to chief pilot to commanding officer, and from an O-3 rank as a new lieutenant to an O-6 as a captain.

What Is the Future Outlook for Aviators?

According to the Bureau of Labor Statistics, opportunities for qualified individuals should remain good through 2022.

What Are Employment Prospects in the Civilian World?

Many pilots make the Coast Guard a career, but those who choose to return to civilian life may be eligible for a commercial pilot's license or instructor's license. They may fly commercial cargo planes or passenger planes. Helicopter pilots may fly news helicopters or become EMS helicopter pilots for hospitals.

Health Services Technician

Health services technicians (HS) provide emergency health care services and basic routine medical care to Coast Guard service members and their families. As part of their jobs, they may assist doctors and dentists, perform diagnostic tests (such as X-rays and lab testing), evaluate and diagnose illness and injury, provide first responder emergency care, prescribe some medications, administer vaccinations, and do minor surgical procedures. An HS may work in a large medical clinic on shore, in a medical bay aboard a cutter, or as the sole health care provider for a crew aboard a vessel or in a small land station. Petty Officer 1st Class Richard Quintana, for example, is the health services technician aboard the Coast Guard cutter *SPAR* out of Kodiak, Alaska. He is the only medical service member on the

At A Glance:
Health Services Technician

Minimal Educational Requirements
High school diploma

Personal Qualities
Able to work closely with others; attention to detail; quick decision maker

Certification and Licensing
CPR and EMT certification

Working Conditions
Medical clinics ashore, duty stations, and aboard cutters at sea

Salary Range
Monthly salary depends on pay grade and years of service

Number of Jobs
About 730

Future Job Outlook
Stable

ship, so he is responsible for running the sickbay and assessing and treating all illnesses and injuries among the fifty crew members. His duties also include enforcing sanitation standards aboard ship and providing mandatory medical educational training for all the crew. He is also the one to decide if an injured or ill crew member has a serious problem that requires evacuation to a medical facility.

Petty Officer 2nd Class Jessica McLeod, on the other hand, works at a large clinic at USCG Base Elizabeth City. She assists medical professionals in providing medical and dental care as well as pharmacy services to Coast Guard personnel. Petty Officer 1st Class William M. Hilt is an HS working out of San Francisco in port security. One of his jobs there was to quickly perform 140 health assessments for service members being deployed in the Middle East for antiterrorism efforts on the seas.

Health services technicians may function as medics, EMT and CPR instructors, suicide responders, and advocates for their fellow crew members with medical issues. They may take on the responsibility of helping other members quit smoking or traveling to remote stations to administer influenza vaccines during an outbreak. When survivors are rescued from emergencies at sea and brought back to Coast Guard stations, health services technicians may be the first to evaluate the victims and determine what medical care is needed.

Once when health services technician Anjelica Hopkins-Slayton was serving aboard the cutter *Dallas* in the Caribbean, her ship intercepted a boat full of eighty Cuban migrants in dire straits. Several of the migrants were severely dehydrated and one was in serious pain. Hopkins-Slayton set up intravenous fluid replacement therapy for these patients and established a morphine drip for the migrant in pain. In an article in the *Military Times* titled "2007 Coast Guard Times Winner: Health Services Technician Anjelica Hopkins-Slayton," Hopkins-Slayton said of the experience, "[It was] something I would never have fathomed doing as a third class. It was extremely exciting. I like being in any situation where there's high drama. I love that. I like being challenged. It's where you find out what you actually know." Health services technicians never know what medical emergencies they may be called upon to handle.

How Do You Become a Health Services Technician?

Education

Health services technicians are enlisted service members with a high school diploma. To prepare for this career, the Coast Guard recommends that high school students take courses such as practical mathematics, anatomy, biology, physiology, and chemistry.

Once a recruit completes basic training and a four-month wait period, he or she may apply to HS "A" School, which has an estimated waiting list time of eighteen to twenty-one months before acceptance. HS "A" School lasts approximately five months. The first six weeks are basic EMT training school, with the first day being CPR certification. Upon successful completion of the EMT training, the curriculum continues with lectures, lab work, clinical experience, and practical exercises. Topics of study include anatomy, physiology, sterilization and aseptic techniques, pharmacology, basic lab test procedures, nursing skills, wound repair, patient examination, and preventive medicine. "A" School education is broad, of necessity, because health services technicians must be able to be the first responders in unpredictable emergency situations, rescues, and any medical situation in which a doctor may not be available.

Upon graduation from "A" School, the service member becomes a petty officer 3rd class, with a Coast Guard rate of E-4. In the Coast Guard, enlisted ranks are called rates, and the rates E-4 through E-6 are petty officer grades. Petty officers are the workforce of the Coast Guard and are trusted with much responsibility and leadership as they acquire hands-on experience. All HS "A" School graduates are obligated to serve on active duty for thirty-five months from the date of graduation.

Certification and Licensing

HS graduates must have CPR certification and successfully pass basic EMT school.

Volunteer Work and Internships

The Coast Guard says that any previous experience in the medical or dental fields is helpful for "A" School admission and success. Anyone interested in an HS career might consider joining a local volunteer rescue squad. Many rescue squads throughout the country have junior programs in which sixteen- and seventeen-year-olds can attend CPR and EMT training, ride along with emergency crews, and help provide medical services to the community. Recruits who already have EMT certification upon joining the Coast Guard are valued and need only recertification in "A" School. Volunteering at a local hospital can be extremely valuable too, whether in a traditional candy striper program or in a junior medic volunteer program. Hospital volunteers may gain experience in clerical fields or interacting with patients. Red Cross volunteers acquire experience in community service and training in areas such as safety, babysitting skills, CPR, first aid, and blood donor drives. All of these experiences can help a young person decide if health services is a good fit for them.

Physical Requirements, Skills, and Personality

Health services technicians must have normal color vision and be between seventeen and twenty-seven years old at the time they apply for training. Because they may be serving on vessels at sea under various assignments, they must also pass physical fitness and swim tests and have basic firearms skills. Because medical emergencies may occur at any time, an HS must be able to stay calm under stress and to act quickly when necessary. Providing medical care to others means that prospective health services technicians must be able to work closely with others, have a pleasing and comfortable personality, and have good communication and interpersonal skills. Good attention to detail is also a must, and a meticulous approach to diagnosis and treatment is critical, as is the confidence to work independently.

On the Job

Working Conditions

Usually a newly graduated HS is first assigned to a large medical clinic on land. There the HS can gain experience while under the supervision of doctors, dentists, nurses, and advanced health services technicians with years of service. After this first assignment, an HS is typically assigned more independent duty at one of the smaller land-based clinics at a station or unit, or the HS may be assigned to a cutter with a sickbay. In either location, the HS is responsible for all the medical needs of the service members in that place. Sometimes an HS is given temporary duty in search-and-rescue missions or as a member of a disaster response team.

For most health services technicians, there is no such thing as a typical day. In a Coast Guard YouTube video about the "Health Services Technician (HS)," Petty Officer Lyndsey Peters describes her job. She says,

> The best part about working in medical care is that no two days are the same. My day can often include anything from laboratory testing, diagnostics, X-rays, prescribing medications, administering immunizations, and in some cases minor surgeries. The average day is often interrupted by emergencies, so flexibility is crucial. . . . At the end of the day, it's a rewarding job.

Earnings

Military pay is standardized and based on the member's enlisted rate and seniority. In addition to basic pay with automatic pay raises every one to two years, all enlisted members are eligible for supplemental payments and allowances, such as combat pay, flight pay, and food and housing allowances.

Opportunities for Advancement

With experience and further training, health services technicians may become chief petty officers, senior chief petty officers, and master chief petty officers, with rates between E-7 and E-9. An HS may attend "C" School for this advanced training in specific areas. Health services technicians may apply for EMT "C" School, EMT recertification, Dental "C" School, and "C" School training as an Independent Duty Health Services (IDHS) technician. Some service members apply to "C" School directly after "A" School, while others apply months or years later.

EMT "C" School is an intensive college-level course compressed into seven weeks of study. EMT certification is established through successfully passing the National Registry of Emergency Medical Technicians (NREMT) examination. For those who are already EMT certified, the EMT recertification course is a requirement to maintain EMT certification. It is a three-day refresher course that ensures that members maintain their skills. Dental "C" School lasts about twenty days and prepares health services technicians to assist Coast Guard dentists. Students learn to read dental charts, operate dental equipment, take dental X-rays, and administer dental first aid. The IDHS "C" School course is a fourteen-week program that includes the EMT or EMT recertification course plus CPR trainer certification, health record maintenance, and many prevention courses, such as suicide prevention and hazardous-waste safety procedures. Students also learn about medical issues as disparate as sanitation and pest issues and battle-wound dressing procedures. Graduates are prepared for independent duty aboard vessels or in land stations, where they may be the only medical personnel available.

Health services technicians may also advance through the "C" School of the Joint Forces Medical Training Center, which is for all military services. This is what Petty Officer 1st Class Jayme Reed did when she became interested in physical therapy. She attended Physical Therapy Specialist "C" School where she learned about rehabilitation for service members with injuries, amputations, burns, and other physical problems. Upon graduation, Reed served at the Cape May Training Center where she worked with recruits who were injured as they worked their way through basic training—a common problem for people pushing themselves to meet the demands of boot camp.

Other health services technicians may attend military "C" Schools to become pharmacy technicians, advanced laboratory technicians, radiographers, or preventive medicine technicians.

What Is the Future Outlook for Health Services Technicians?

About 730 enlisted personnel currently serve in the health care fields in the Coast Guard. The Coast Guard is a highly selective military service and its retention rate is high, but the Bureau of Labor Statistics predicts that opportunities for qualified individuals should remain good through 2022.

What Are Employment Prospects in the Civilian World?

According to the occupational information site O*NetOnLine.org, the prospects for health services technicians moving into the civilian world are bright. Some of the jobs available include X-ray technician, medical laboratory technician, physician's assistant, practical nurse, and medical assistant.

Damage Controlman

A damage controlman (DC) has many practical skills. He or she is trained to repair and maintain almost anything on a vessel and respond to almost any emergency. At shore stations on land, damage controlmen perform construction and building maintenance. At sea, under normal circumstances, the DC is a plumber, welder, and carpenter, fixing anything that malfunctions or breaks on the ship, from a nonflushing toilet to a damaged shelf in the galley. At the same time, the DC is responsible for any breaches in the watertight integrity of a vessel. For example, in a case of damage to a vessel, watertight closures such as doors and hatches must be secured to prevent and limit flooding. If a fire breaks out, the DC knows what to do to protect the ship and the crew. DCs are experts in shipboard damage control and firefighting and know how to maintain all emergency equipment. They must also know how to perform chemical, radiological, or nuclear decontamination. In sum, a damage controlman is a problem solver with the skills

At A Glance:
Damage Controlman

Minimum Educational Requirements
High school diploma

Personal Qualities
High mechanical aptitude; interest in construction and repair

Certification and Licensing
None

Working Conditions
Engineering rooms aboard vessels or at land stations

Salary Range
Monthly salary depends on pay grade and years of service

Number of Jobs
Approximately 1,200 positions in engineering, science, and technical jobs (including DCs) available

Future Job Outlook
Stable

During a training exercise, a damage controlman aboard the US Coast Guard cutter Stratton *uses a pipe wrench to adjust a fitting. Damage controlmen must be skilled in welding, plumbing, carpentry, and firefighting.*

of many different trades and expertise in emergency repair. When an alarm bell sounds, the damage controlman is the one who responds.

Petty Officer 3rd Class Ryan Wenzel, for example, is one of two damage controlmen serving aboard the cutter *Active*. His job includes weekly, monthly, and yearly inspections of all damage control and fire-fighting equipment, including fire pumps, fire hoses, fire extinguishers, drains, valves, seals, hatches, and pipes. He also trains the rest of the crew in how to respond to a fire or other emergency. At the same time, he is the person the crew turns to whenever anything breaks and needs repair. In a 2015 *Coast Guard Compass* article written by Petty Officer Katelyn Shearer titled "Honor, Respect, Devotion to Duty: DC3 Ryan Wenzel," Wenzel says, "I like being the go-to guy when something breaks. Any task from a little tiny thing to a big project helps the crew."

DCs may have to be creative when things go wrong aboard ship. In 2013, for instance, Petty Officer 3rd Class Marilyn A. Brammer was serving as the damage controlman on the Coast Guard cutter *Oak* when the ship met a Dominican Republic patrol boat in trouble. The patrol boat's engine cooling system was damaged, and it was not straining out the debris in the sea water used to cool the engines. No replacement sea water strainers were available, so Brammer spent three days designing and making three strainers from the pipes and other materials she had on hand in her machine shop. Once the replacement strainers were installed, the patrol boat's engines performed perfectly. In the *Coast Guard Compass* article "There to Fix It," written by Petty Officer Christopher Okula, Brammer remarks, "One of the things I love about being in the Coast Guard is we're always in the unique position to help other people. As a [damage controlman], my job is to basically fabricate things that are needed around the ship. If something breaks or needs modification, we're there to fix it. We're there to create something new. I gain immense satisfaction out of that."

How Do You Become a Damage Controlman?

Education

Damage controlmen are enlisted service members with a high school diploma. Once a recruit completes basic training, he or she is required to wait four months while serving his or her first unit assignment. After that, the seaman may apply to Damage Controlman "A" School, a fifteen-week course that prepares students to be junior petty officers with a damage controlman rating. Some of the basic skills taught include welding, plumbing and pipe fitting, carpentry and construction, watertight closure maintenance, and shipboard firefighting.

Upon graduation from "A" School, the service member becomes a petty officer 3rd class, with a Coast Guard rate of E-4. In the Coast Guard, enlisted ranks are called rates, and the rates E-4 through E-6 are petty officer grades. Petty officers are the technical workforce of the Coast Guard. Throughout their careers, DCs have the opportunity to take on more responsibilities and training and advance through the petty officer rates.

Certification and Licensing

No licensing is required for this job, but because sea duty is expected, DCs must be able to pass a standardized twelve-minute swim test.

Volunteer Work and Internships

Although not required, the Coast Guard recommends any prior experience in welding, carpentry, plumbing, or firefighting as helpful to those who want to become damage controlmen. Interested students might join a local volunteer fire department. Many fire departments throughout the country offer firefighter volunteer programs. Parental consent is required for those under eighteen years of age, and all volunteers must have a driver's license. Working with family members who are plumbers, carpenters, or welders could also benefit students interested in this career. Volunteers with organizations such as Habitat for Humanity can learn basic construction skills while helping others.

Physical Requirements, Skills, and Personality

DCs need a high mechanical aptitude, good hand-eye coordination, and an interest in construction and repair. They should enjoy working with their hands and solving practical problems. At the same time, damage controlmen need to be able to respond calmly and quickly to emergencies. DCs achieve satisfaction from building and creating, often under challenging circumstances and with limited materials. In a video for the website Today'sMilitary.com, damage controlman Petty Officer 1st Class Timothy Florez-Adams describes the personal qualities that make him a success at his job. He says, "We're basically the jack-of-all-trades. I support everyone on the boat from the CO [commanding officer] all the way down to the smallest non-rate [enlisted personnel without a specified career path]. I have to work with everybody. . . . It's a constant battle for me because little things add up, and the responsibility does get overwhelming sometimes." Even under difficult circumstances, the DC is dedicated to functioning competently and professionally.

On the Job

Working Conditions

Damage controlmen serve onshore and aboard vessels throughout the Coast Guard, including in Alaska, Hawaii, Puerto Rico, and Guam. Wherever they are assigned, however, there is no such thing as a typical day. DCs can be found on all cutters, river tenders, icebreakers, and buoy tenders throughout the Coast Guard, and they may be at sea for months at a time. Aboard ship they are assigned to the engineering department. That means that in addition to their shop duties of maintenance and repair they are expected to be able to stand engineering watch, making sure everything is running smoothly. DCs on vessels do not have 9-to-5 jobs. They have to be ready to fix anything that breaks at any time. In any emergency the DC responds no matter what time of day or night. At the same time the DC regularly is in charge of training the rest of the crew in firefighting, fire safety, and emergency response to major ship damage and flooding.

Seagoing DCs are the experts who also fix the vessel's plumbing and septic systems. Shipboard plumbing frequently needs maintenance. However, as damage controlman Petty Officer 2nd Class Christina Butler says on the Coast Guard's Facebook page video, a DC does much more than plumbing. He or she has a job of constant variety, including welding, firefighting, and working in the engine room. Butler says, "I learn something new every day."

Damage controlmen assigned to land stations, on the other hand, are likely to work normal daily schedules most of the time. Onshore stations may include Integrated Support Commands (large operating bases), air stations, marine safety offices, tactical law enforcement units, and small boat stations. Some DCs may work at stations on construction and repair of station facilities and housing units for Coast Guard members. Chief Petty Officer Dennis Amerson has another kind of job. He is assigned to the Coast Guard Yard in Baltimore, Maryland. It is the Coast Guard's only shipyard where construction, repair, and renovation take place for all the Coast Guard's fleet. Amerson leads the Yard Fire Department, which provides fire protection and emergency medical, hazardous material, and environmental response for the entire shipyard. Chief Warrant Officer Jason Briggs works at the engineering facility for the Coast Guard Training Center at Petaluma, California, where he is in charge of maintenance and repair for the whole center. Petty Officer 1st Class Robert Somers is assigned to an air station in Clearwater, Florida, where he works a fairly regular schedule and has time for local volunteer work and involvement with the community. The machinery technician shop at Clearwater provides welding, carpentry, plumbing, and general repair and renovation for the base. The Coast Guard says that damage controlmen have some of the most interesting and diverse working conditions available anywhere.

Earnings

Military pay is standardized and based on the member's enlisted rate and seniority. In addition to basic pay with automatic pay raises every one to two years, all enlisted members are eligible for supplemental payments and allowances, such as combat pay, flight pay, and food and housing allowances. Pay also increases with each rate promotion, such as from E-4 to E-5.

Opportunities for Advancement

With experience and further training, DCs may become chief petty officers, senior chief petty officers, and master chief petty officers with rates between E-7 and E-9. A damage controlman may attend "C" School for this advanced training. Some may apply to "C" School directly after finishing "A" School; others may apply months or even years later. At "C" School, DCs get advanced, mostly hands-on training in steel welding, aluminum welding, firefighting, and ship damage control. The course for aluminum welding, for example, lasts about twenty days and emphasizes safety, troubleshooting, and operation of gas metal arc and gas tungsten arc welding. To graduate, DCs are required to be able to weld in flat, horizontal, vertical, and overhead positions and to produce a weldment free of defects. To become a DC repair leader involves a further two-week course in firefighting and shipboard damage repair.

Senior enlisted members (chief petty officers with rates of E-7 through E-9) may get advanced training in leadership and damage control training in firefighting and ship survivability in a thirty-five-day course that includes college-level information in environmental hazards instrumentation and in ship safety. The training prepares these members for senior damage control leadership positions aboard vessels.

What Is the Future Outlook for Damage Controlmen?

Damage controlmen are considered part of the engineering staff in the Coast Guard. As of 2013 there were 1,272 active duty enlisted service members in the engineering, science, and technical occupations in the Coast Guard. The Coast Guard is a highly selective military service and its retention rate is high, but according to the Bureau of Labor Statistics, opportunities for qualified individuals in damage control should remain good through 2022.

What Are Employment Prospects in the Civilian World?

The Coast Guard Training Center Yorktown points out on its website, "A single Damage Controlman in today's Coast Guard has the knowledge and skills of numerous civilian professional trades." Some of the jobs available to a DC in the civilian world include firefighter, welder, plumber, carpenter, pipefitter, and ship fitter. Other possibilities include construction foreman, trade school teacher, home inspector, building inspector, maintenance supervisor, and safety engineer.

Marine Science Technician

At A Glance:
Marine Science Technician

Minimum Educational Requirements
High school diploma

Personal Qualities
Interest in the environment; science and math aptitude

Certification and Licensing
None

Working Conditions
At shore stations, in harbor patrols, and on ships

Salary Range
Monthly salary depends on pay grade and years of service

Number of Jobs
About 1,200

Future Job Outlook
Steady

A marine science technician's (MST) job is to ensure marine environmental safety and protect the waters and the public from pollution and other hazards. A large part of this job is law enforcement because enforcing regulations helps keep the oceans safe and ports secure. In law enforcement, MSTs may have a variety of job responsibilities. Marine science technicians have to know environmental law, recognize violations of those laws, and take responsibility for preventing violations of shipping laws and regulations. An MST may serve as a vessel inspection officer or port control officer. In this position, the MST boards and inspects vessels to determine that they are complying with US laws and international treaties in terms of structural stability; electrical, navigational, and mechanical systems; fire safety; and crew living conditions. These inspections include commercial fishing boats, cargo ships, and passenger vessels—both foreign and domestic—traveling in US waters. MSTs perform harbor patrols as well, to keep harbors and ports safe from hazards and secure from threats and to watch for any pollution evidence. In port, MSTs inspect commercial waterfront facilities and shipping containers. They check for hazardous materials and structural integrity of containers holding hazardous materials. They must check petroleum-based products (such as oil, propane, and liquid gas) carried on vessels and certify that the cargo is transported according to safety regulations as well as supervise the loading and unloading of explosives.

Marine science technicians may also be responsible for investigating pollution incidents or supervising the cleanup of a pollution accident. They may discover a marine pest species on a foreign ship (such as the zebra mussels inadvertently released into the Great Lakes in 1988) and thereby prevent its establishment or spread in US waters. In the event of a major oil spill or natural disaster, MSTs respond and know how to set up a disaster-response plan and put that plan into action. So in addition to enforcement of environmental safety laws, the MST has scientific knowledge related to remediation of hazardous material spills and also to weather and how weather patterns affect responses to ocean pollution. He or she may be called upon to conduct a chemical analysis of a water sample or pollutant, use scientific instruments to conduct oceanic or weather observations, and record data in logs or charts.

Every year a few MSTs are chosen to work on the icebreakers that are committed to the Coast Guard's scientific research in the Arctic and Antarctic. On these coveted assignments, marine science technicians assist the scientists investigating ice cores, marine life, and environmental health in polar regions. On the large research cutters, MSTs might be called upon to collect weather data or information on sea ice conditions and report their findings to the National Weather Service. They might assist in scientific collection of water or animal samples—from plankton to vampire squid. On-the-job scientific learning is always available to MSTs as they fulfill their duties on the icebreakers devoted to research.

How Do You Become a Marine Science Technician?

Education

Marine science technicians are enlisted service members with a high school diploma. In preparation for this career, the Coast Guard recommends that students take any courses in environmental sciences. In addition, courses in algebra, trigonometry, chemistry, and physics are useful.

Once a recruit completes basic training and four months of basic sea duty, he or she may apply to Marine Science Technician "A" School. The wait time for most service members to be accepted into MST "A" School is about two years. The school is nine weeks long and covers the basic skills needed to become an entry-level MST and a junior petty officer. According to the Coast Guard "A" School information website, topics covered include occupational health and safety; port safety and security; commercial vessel inspections; waterfront facilities inspections; dangerous cargo stowage and segregation; marine environmental response; enforcement of domestic and international law.

Upon graduation from "A" School, the service member becomes a Petty Officer 3rd Class, with a Coast Guard rate of E-4. In the Coast Guard, enlisted ranks are called rates, and the grades E-4 through E-6 are petty officer rates. Petty officers are the technical workforce of the Coast Guard. Throughout their careers, with experience and further training, MSTs have the opportunity to take on more responsibilities and advance through the petty officer rates.

Certification and Licensing

Entry level MSTs require no certification. Advanced level MSTs can achieve certification as a facility inspector, port state control officer, or pollution responder.

Volunteer Work and Internships

The Coast Guard considers any experience in environmental sciences helpful for the MST rating. Many nonprofit environmental protection organizations such as the Nature Conservancy or Earthwatch offer volunteer opportunities for interested individuals. The US Environmental Protection Agency (EPA) lists many citizen volunteer opportunities for helping to protect the nation's waters and coastlines. The EPA has a volunteer water monitoring program, for instance, through which individuals can receive training and then assess conditions in streams, waterways, lakes, and wetlands; identify problems; report data to the EPA; and help clean up and prevent pollution.

Skills and Personality

MSTs have a strong interest in protecting and saving the marine environment. They enjoy the excitement and adventure of a seagoing experience. Because they do so much boarding and inspection, marine science technicians have to be good at dealing with people and still have the attention to detail necessary to carrying out their investigations. They need to be good at math and science but also be able to learn and understand federal laws and regulations. An MST must have the skills to calculate the area of an oil spill on water or the flow rates of liquids in pipes. He or she must figure out the maximum cargo and passenger weight that a vessel can carry and still be stable or determine if the rust damage on the hull of a ship threatens its safety. At the same time, MSTs need the verbal and writing skills to issue detailed citations or even initiate a federal lawsuit against a party responsible for a pollution incident. In sum an MST has a wide variety of skills.

On the Job

Working Conditions

Marine science technicians work on cutters and icebreakers, from patrol boats out of air stations and other land stations on the waterfront, and out of large sector bases. In addition, some MSTs are stationed at the Marine Safety Lab (which provides forensic analysis of pollution) and at the International Ice Patrol (which monitors icebergs in the North Atlantic), both of which are in New London, Connecti-

A marine science technician aboard the US Coast Guard cutter Polar Star *collects and treats South Pacific sea water samples. Marine science technicians ensure marine environmental safety and protect the waters and the public from pollution and other hazards.*

cut. Throughout their careers, marine science technicians are likely to have an extensive number of different assignments and missions. They work wherever their skills are needed to protect the environment. Newly graduated MSTs are first assigned to units where they can get on-the-job training and experience under other MSTs, whether in handling hazardous materials; performing pollution cleanups; patrolling harbors; or inspecting port facilities, shipping containers, and cargo and commercial vessels.

While on duty onshore, MSTs often have to be ready to don protective hazmat suits, coveralls, gloves, face gear, and hard hats to perform their investigations of hazardous materials. They also have to know how to decontaminate themselves and their gear when necessary. They wear protective suits, gloves, and footwear when they are in a polluted environment, too, as they work on an oil cleanup or investigate unknown substances on a fouled beach. But the daily inspections of onshore commercial facilities to prevent pollution are just as much a part of an MST's job as the cleanups. Petty Officer Will Khams, for example, is stationed at the Coast Guard Marine Safety Unit Morgan City, Louisiana, where commercial oil is big business. He inspects the facilities of the oil port. In an article titled "A Safer, Cleaner Tomorrow" for the *Coast Guard Heartland* blog, Khams told writer Carlos Vega, "We inspect facilities to make sure they are in compliance with applicable federal regulations to prevent pollution. A lot of our regulations have to do with inspecting the hoses that transfer oil from the facility to the vessel." The working conditions for Khams and the other MSTs at their unit are not arduous, but all of them are proud of protecting the safety of people and the environment.

Other MSTs work out of Coast Guard Sector Juneau in Alaska, checking containers being shipped on the ocean while wearing protective gear. Some work on recording weather and iceberg observations for the International Ice Patrol. Still others spend most of their time in harbor patrol boats, intercepting and inspecting incoming vessels, perhaps in California, New York, or Baltimore. Some work out of the National Strike Force, which has its coordination center in Elizabeth City, North Carolina. They are part of the nation's rapidly deployable response team, ready to respond to any environmental disaster or public health emergency at any place and any time.

Earnings

Military pay is standardized and based on the member's enlisted rate and seniority. In addition to basic pay with automatic pay raises every one to two years, all enlisted members are eligible for supplemental payments and allowances, such as combat pay, flight pay, and food and housing allowances.

Opportunities for Advancement

During their Coast Guard careers, marine science technicians usually return to school several times for advanced training. This training may be for cargo container inspection, commercial fishing vessel safety, explosives handling, port security, and antiterrorism techniques. These training sessions are generally about one or two weeks long, and at their conclusion the service member is certified through examination as competent for port state control, container inspection, facilities inspection, or other specialized duties. MSTs who have completed "A" School may attend a Marine Science Technician Second Class course and a Marine Science Technician First Class course as well. Those assigned to icebreakers, air stations, and the International Ice Patrol can receive advanced training in weather forecasting at the Joint Service Weather Training Facility at Keesler Air Force Base, Biloxi, Mississippi. MSTs assigned to icebreakers are eligible for advanced on-the-job training in oceanography from the University-National Oceanographic Laboratory System, which allows them to serve on different university research vessels anywhere in the world doing oceanographic research. Senior enlisted members (chief petty officers with rates of E-7 through E-9) who have acquired college credits and degrees are always eligible to apply to Officer Candidate School and continue their Coast Guard careers as officers.

What Is the Future Outlook for Marine Science Technicians?

About 1,200 active-duty marine science technicians serve in the Coast Guard currently. The Coast Guard is a highly selective service, and the retention rate is high, but according to the Bureau of Labor Statistics, opportunities for qualified individuals in marine science should remain good through 2022.

What Are Employment Prospects in the Civilian World?

People with marine science training and knowledge and experience in protecting the environment are in demand in the civilian world. Some of the civilian jobs to which MSTs are suited include vessel inspector, hazardous material specialist, oil spill responder, marine safety specialist, and marine environmental specialist.

Operations Specialist

What Does an Operations Specialist Do?

Operations specialists (OS) are the technical experts in the fields of tactical command, control, and communications. The website Go CoastGuard.com refers to operations specialists as "the eyes, ears and voice of the Coast Guard for the maritime community." The site explains, "OSs operate the most advanced tactical computer systems the Coast Guard has, to include satellite communications, global positions navigation, electronic charting, shipboard navigation systems, and real-time target acquisition tracking and identification systems." Commonly working onshore at command centers or aboard large cutters, operations specialists receive and distribute information through communications systems worldwide. They are responsible for point-to-point voice and data communications and also monitor radio frequencies dedicated to distress calls from both professional and recreational boaters.

OSs may not be the service

At A Glance:

Operations Specialist

Minimum Educational Requirements
High school diploma

Personal Qualities
Computer and math aptitude; calm in emergencies; good communicator

Certification and Licensing
Security clearance

Working Conditions
Standing watch in communication and command centers aboard ships and on land

Salary Range
Monthly salary depends on pay grade and years of service

Number of Jobs
Operations specialists are currently in demand

Future Job Outlook
Good

members who board a smuggler's vessel to seize contraband or the rescue swimmers who leap into the ocean to save a life, but they are an essential part of every mission the Coast Guard undertakes. In 2015, for example, the Coast Guard cutter *Stratton* was on a months-long law enforcement mission in the eastern Pacific. In the operations center, OSs stood watch, monitoring computer screens, radar, radio transmissions, and communications from other Coast Guard vessels and aircraft, as well as from international partners and other military branch vessels. A transmission came in from a patrol aircraft, reporting that a semisubmersible sea craft had been spotted. These submarine-like vessels are a favorite tool of international criminal drug smugglers, and they are difficult to spot. Once the OS on duty received and relayed the transmission and the coordinates, the *Stratton* was able to intercept the craft. Small boats, a helicopter, and boarding teams were deployed from the cutter, and the *Stratton* was able to seize the vessel and its crew, along with 8.4 tons (7.6 metric tons) of cocaine. Coordinating the efforts by relaying information, communications, and positions of all the Coast Guard team were the operations specialists in the command center.

Operations specialists are just as critical to search-and-rescue missions. In command centers onshore, OSs often function like 911 emergency operators for maritime rescue, receiving distress and Mayday calls, getting the information, and transmitting that information to those who can help. OSs set rescues in motion. Petty Officer 1st Class Stacy Slavinski, for instance, is an operations specialist at Coast Guard Sector New York. She is featured in a video titled "Voice of the Coast Guard," produced by the Public Affairs Detachment of New York about Coast Guard operations specialists for the website DVIDS (Defense Video & Imagery Distribution System). She says, "You're dealing with people's lives. You're dealing with frantic callers on the other end of a radio call, so you have to keep your head and keep calm. Basically be the calm voice for them in a panic situation."

Slavinski is proud to be part of a team that does everything it can to rescue people in desperate situations. She describes participating in a search-and-rescue operation to locate missing swimmers. Other OSs describe sending out general broadcasts about pleasure boats in need of a tow so that any vessel in the area can respond or directing

Coast Guard vessels to the location of a vessel on fire. One OS described receiving several distress calls from recreational boaters who saw a small sea plane crash and overturn in a bay. He had to coordinate that response and ensure that the pilot was rescued.

How Do You Become an Operations Specialist?

Education

Operations specialists are enlisted service members with a high school diploma. Once a recruit completes basic training, most are required to wait four months while serving a first unit assignment before applying for "A" School training for a specific job. This requirement is waived for service members wishing to become operations specialists, as the job is in high demand.

Operations Specialist "A" School is seventeen weeks long and covers the basic skills needed to become an entry level OS and a junior petty officer. At OS "A" School, students learn to determine locations using longitude and latitude; they learn to use all the technology in an Operations Center, including communication systems and software applications for search and rescue, navigation, and tactical operations; they are trained in standing a watch at a command center and taking and responding to maritime distress calls.

Upon graduation from "A" School, the service member becomes a Petty Officer 3rd Class, with a Coast Guard rate of E-4. In the Coast Guard, enlisted ranks are called rates, and the grades E-4 through E-6 are petty officer rates. Petty officers are the technical workforce of the Coast Guard. Throughout their careers, with experience and further training, OSs have the opportunity to take on more responsibilities and advance through the petty officer rates.

Certification and Licensing

An OS must hold a security clearance or a top security clearance, depending on his or her assignment and the kind of secret national security information he or she will handle.

Volunteer Work and Internships

The Coast Guard recommends any aptitude or experience with computer-based applications as helpful for this job. Working as an intern in any IT (information technology) company or in a university computer science program might be valuable for people interested in an OS career. In addition (although not required), any college credits in computer science would be valuable. Informal experience with software applications such as spreadsheets and word processing is a benefit, as might be volunteering with a local emergency or rescue squad for the experience of handling emergency situations.

Physical Requirements, Skills, and Personality

Operations specialists are required to have normal hearing and color vision. They must be US citizens and be eligible for a security clearance. At the website GoCoastGuard.com, the Coast Guard says of the qualifications for operations specialists, "You should have the ability to work in a stressful and high-paced environment, interest and aptitudes for working with computer-based applications, exceptional attention to detail and above average ability in solving mathematical problems." An operations specialist has a variety of skills. He or she is good with computers, good with communications, good at working with people, and good at taking control in emergency situations.

OSs typically enjoy the fast-paced and high-stress nature of their jobs. They relish making quick decisions, coping with the demands of being the information hub for their team, and remaining calm under pressure. Many of them say that the ability to remain calm no matter what, even when dealing with panicked people, is a critical personal characteristic. Operations specialists take pride in knowing they are helping people and that they are instrumental in accomplishing any mission. OSs tend to be about equally divided between land and sea assignments, but many of them particularly want to be assigned to the cutters because they want to travel and enjoy the time and adventure at sea.

On the Job

Working Conditions

Whether stationed at an onshore command center, operations center, or aboard ship, operations specialists can expect to work in windowless rooms, staring at computer screens, radar screens, and other assorted equipment screens for hours at a time. Every OS has to get used to the intense focus this work requires because most OSs are watch standers throughout their careers. A watch stander is a service member assigned for a certain length of time to the task of keeping watch over various instruments and equipment and identifying any situation that requires a response. An OS must cope with both the pressure and the attentional demands of watch standing. Petty Officer 1st Class Jeremy Young, for instance, is an OS at an onshore operations center. He considers his job both important and rewarding, but the working conditions are not easy. In a 2013 *Coast Guard Compass* article titled "Got Questions? These Operations Specialists Have Answers," Young says, "Your eyes get dry and stressed out, but you power through it. You don't literally stare at a computer screen for eight to twelve hours; you talk to watchstanders, read a pub or manual so you can be that subject expert. On a ship, the good watch supervisors will relieve the radar watchstander for a break as needed."

Operations specialists are shift workers because operations centers must function twenty-four hours a day. Different OSs in different duty stations will work varied watch rotations, depending on the personnel available and the needs of the operations center. Young, for instance, says that he worked twelve-hour shifts, with three days on duty and then three days off. An OS never knows what kind of shift duty—day or night—he or she will need to serve, but sometimes the schedule can feel long and challenging.

While on watch duty, most communications an OS receives and transmits are nondistress, but in an instant that situation can change. An important component of an OS's working conditions is the need to be alert to and prepared for an emergency communication at any time. Chief Petty Officer Nick Ameen writes in "Standing the Mid-Watch" for the *Coast Guard Compass*, "Coast Guard men and women in command centers across the country are standing the watch, ready for the call. Whether it's noon or midnight, the watch never stops ticking."

Earnings

Military pay is standardized and based on the member's enlisted rate and seniority. In addition to basic pay with automatic pay raises every one to two years, all enlisted members are eligible for supplemental payments and allowances, such as combat pay, flight pay, and food and housing allowances. Operations specialists may also be eligible for an enlistment bonus or a reenlistment bonus, depending on budget constraints.

Opportunities for Advancement

With experience and on-the-job training, OSs may become chief petty officers, senior chief petty officers, and master chief petty officers with rates between E-7 and E-9. With advancement in rate, an OS may become the watch supervisor, and with a top secret security clearance, conduct top secret telephone, Internet, and radio communications. With further education, experience, and required sea duty, operations specialists may also advance to warrant officers. Some operations specialists may earn commissions as officers as they work over time with command staff and operations.

What Is the Future Outlook for Operations Specialists?

Operations specialists are in demand as the Coast Guard does not have enough personnel in this job. The Coast Guard is actively looking for qualified individuals to serve as operations specialists, both through enlistment of new recruits and for any personnel already in the Coast Guard or those who have been enlisted in any other branch of the military.

What Are Employment Prospects in the Civilian World?

Many OSs make the Coast Guard a career, but those who choose to return to civilian life may qualify for jobs such as city or state emergency operations coordinator, air or vessel traffic controller, database manager, or intelligence analyst.

Sector Commander

What Does a Sector Commander Do?

In the Coast Guard organization, there are thirty-five shore-based, geographical sectors around the country and in US territories. Sectors are large operational units that are responsible for executing all missions within the sector's area of responsibility. Within each sector are the stations, facilities, vessels, and air stations where Coast Guard operations are carried out. The commanding officer of the sector is the sector commander who is in charge of search-and-rescue missions, security and safety of the coastal waters and inland waterways, law enforcement, and maritime inspections. A sector commander is the captain of the port, the federal maritime security coordinator, the officer in charge of marine inspections, the search-and-rescue mission coordinator, and the federal on-scene coordinator.

A sector commander has a lot of responsibility. As captain of the port, for example, the sector commander is ultimately responsible for tracking all vessels, their movements, and anchorages; preventing pollution; overseeing the safe transport or

At A Glance:
Sector Commander

Minimum Educational Requirements
Advanced academic degree

Personal Qualities
Leadership and command ability; teamwork and communication skills; devotion to duty

Rank
Captain

Working Conditions
At sector command centers onshore

Salary Range
Monthly salary depends on pay grade and years of service

Number of Jobs
Thirty-five

Future Job Outlook
Stable but highly competitive

transfer of explosives or chemical hazards; and preventing any damage to any vessel, port, or harbor facility. In the case of an accident or incident, the sector commander is the federal on-scene coordinator who evaluates the magnitude of the problem, oversees the response and cleanup to determine that it is appropriate and successful, and makes the decision that the cleanup is finished so that the mission can be terminated. As the officer in charge of marine inspections, the sector commander administers and enforces all regulations of vessels, harbor and port facilities, and shipyards. He or she is responsible for investigating any injuries or deaths to people aboard commercial and recreational vessels and has the authority to suspend or revoke licenses and certificates for misconduct or misbehavior. As the search-and-rescue coordinator, the sector commander knows and follows all Coast Guard policies for the missions and also has the authority and knowledge to determine when to suspend a search.

Sector commanders are in charge of a large amount of territory and in command of a lot of Coast Guard personnel. The sector commander of Coast Guard Sector Northern New England, for instance, is responsible for 5,100 miles (8,207 km) of coastline and 540 service members. Coast Guard Sector Anchorage is an even larger territory, covering 35,000 miles (56,327 km) of coastline and 4,000 miles (6,437 km) of rivers. Coast Guard Sector New York has more than 700 active-duty Coast Guard members and 300 members of the Coast Guard reserve—all under the leadership of the sector commander.

How Do You Become a Sector Commander?

Education

A sector commander is a career officer, usually with the rank of captain, who has a college bachelor's degree and an advanced academic degree. The Coast Guard offers several different paths to becoming an officer and rising in the ranks to captaincy and sector commander. Some attend the Coast Guard Academy in New London, Connecticut. It is a four-year college program that also prepares cadets to become junior officers—ensigns—upon graduation. The eight academic majors offered at the academy are civil engineering, electrical engineering, mechanical engineering, naval architecture/marine engineering, operations research/computer analysis, marine and environmental sciences, management, and government.

Others become officers by attending Officer Candidate School (OCS) after graduating from college. OCS is seventeen weeks of intense instruction in military lifestyle, leadership, physical training, navigation, ship's operations, and seamanship. Upon graduation, these service members are newly commissioned ensigns. As they continue in their Coast Guard careers and with further education, these officers may have a variety of academic qualifications, with advanced degrees in areas such as law, environmental management, national security and strategic studies, or geography and marine affairs. The Coast Guard offers a tuition assistance program for all members wishing to further their education.

Other sector commanders begin their careers as enlisted service members, perhaps as a health services technician or a boatswain's mate. With college degrees earned either before or after enlistment, these enlisted members go on to OCS, become officers, continue their education, and advance in their ranks. No matter which path service members take to become officers, the Coast Guard offers them continual opportunities for further training and academic specialization throughout their careers.

Military Qualification

Perhaps much more important than educational background for rising in the Coast Guard ranks to sector commander is an officer's accomplishments, experience, and dedication to the Coast Guard's values and mission. The official website GoCoastGuard.com explains, "Officers selected for promotion will have demonstrated the leadership traits, core values (honor, respect, devotion to duty) and performance that confirm their potential to serve in positions of increased responsibility." Newly commissioned officers are ensigns, with a grade of O-1. Grades between O-1 through O-10 are officer ratings. The progression from ensign, with certain defined years of service for each promotional consideration, is to junior lieutenant (O-2), lieutenant (O-3), lieutenant commander (O-4), commander (O-5), captain (O-6), and ranks of admirals (O-7 through O-10).

On average, the time needed to achieve the job of sector commander is twenty-two years or more. During these years, the officers have taken on greater and greater responsibilities with each new assignment. They have experienced extensive on-the-job training and taken advantage of those opportunities. Most serve as deputy sector commanders (second in command) before achieving their own Sector Command. In addition, those captains who become sector commanders usually have specialized during their careers in onshore marine safety and security.

Skills and Personality

Perhaps the most important attributes of people who become sector commanders are leadership qualities, the ability to shoulder responsibility, and a career-long job performance that is above and beyond expectations or requirements. In the case of an emergency, the sector commander has to have the ability to act independently and make far-reaching decisions because he or she has broad Coast Guard authority to take any necessary actions without authorization from more senior people, either federally or within the Coast Guard structure. A sector commander has the confidence and the knowledge to accept a lot of responsibility in several different areas and make decisions about the safety, security, and stewardship of waterways that define the Coast Guard's functions. In sum, a sector commander has to have the personality to be able to skillfully take charge.

Sector commanders also have to be highly skilled at working with others, communicating, and being part of a team. They are often called upon to coordinate Coast Guard activities with other military branches, civilian police or firefighters, or different federal agencies. During Hurricane Sandy in 2012, for example, Captain Gordon Loebl, commander of Sector New York, worked to coordinate the preparation and response with several city agencies. In a 2014 interview with reporter Ken Kraetzer for Sons of the American Legion Radio and posted on You Tube, titled "USCG Captain Gordon Loebl, NY Sector Commander," he says of the hurricane response effort, "To see everybody just roll up their sleeves, pull together, get to work, do what had to be done. . . . It just made me very proud to be in the Coast Guard."

In a 2007 paper titled "Developing a Career as a Coast Guard Officer" and published online for the USCG officer corps, the Coast Guard lists three main characteristics of successful captains in the service. It says, in part,

- Successful captains should have had the opportunity to show they can improve and sustain mission execution at their units. Those having held command in the grade of captain have demonstrated performance that includes managing risk, achieving results, and leading large and complex organizations. . . .
- Successful captains should also understand how the Coast Guard works within the broader governmental picture . . . and have political savvy.
- Officers at this level should have exposure to areas of expertise outside the Coast Guard, and to develop a persona that brings external skills, abilities, and perspectives to the service.

Because the Coast Guard is a small, multi-mission organization, a sector commander has to have the multitude of skills and personal qualities that make effective leadership and decision making possible. Like all career Coast Guard officers, sector commanders love the service and are dedicated to its values and its missions.

On the Job

Working Conditions

Sector commanders work onshore in one of the Sector Command centers around the United States or its territories. Their positions are basically executive and administrative. This means, for example, receiving daily operational briefings, overseeing and supervising all the service members assigned to the sector, attending conferences and meetings about sector operations, writing and submitting operational reports, and planning and approving responses or delegating authority for search-and-rescue missions, accident investigations, and law enforcement operations.

The sector commander often serves as the voice of the Coast Guard, informing the public of operations, giving interviews with the media, and explaining Coast Guard functions. He or she also works to coordinate Coast Guard missions with other agencies. As the commander of Sector Miami, for example, Captain Austin Gould partners with the US Customs and Border Protection agency and co-ordinates security efforts. In an online article for GSN (Government Security News) titled "Austin Gould, Commander of Coast Guard Sector Miami, Describes Mission Challenges, New Initiatives," he explains, "We go through a morning brief. Where are they flying and where are we flying[?] Where are they going to patrol[?] In this day and age you can't afford to duplicate efforts." The needs of each sector are different, and the sector commander establishes the priorities and supervises all the missions for which the sector is responsible. A sector commander's days can be strenuous and exacting, requiring the devotion to duty for which the Coast Guard is known.

Earnings

Military pay is standardized and based on the member's officer rank and seniority. In addition, officers receive housing and living allowances, medical and dental coverage, paid vacation, life insurance, and medical benefits.

Opportunities for Advancement

The Coast Guard is organized into two overall areas—the Atlantic area and the Pacific area. Within these regions, it is further organized into nine districts, with various numbers of sectors within each district. The district commander is a rear admiral lower half—a one star flag officer. (All admirals are called "flag officers.") Promotion to rear admiral is an extremely selective process, with only about thirty-eight rear admirals altogether in the Coast Guard. Captains who achieve the rank of rear admiral lower half have been recommended by a board of active flag officers and selected by the president of the United States with the advice and consent of the Senate. Captains who are sector commanders may be promoted to rear admiral lower half and assigned to be district commanders.

What Is the Future Outlook for Sector Commanders?

With twenty-two years of service and three years at the rank of captain, the best qualified 50 percent of captains have the opportunity for promotion. Captains (at the rank of O-6) face mandatory retirement after thirty years if not on the list for promotion, or at the age of sixty-two. These requirements mean that new positions for incoming captains and sector commanders routinely open up for the most qualified individuals.

What Are Employment Prospects in the Civilian World?

At the level of captain, sector commanders are career officers who retire to the civilian world, with honor and retirement pay. They have no need to seek employment in civilian life.

Interview with a Sector Commander

Captain Claudia C. Gelzer is a sector commander in the US Coast Guard. She is the commander of Coast Guard Sector Boston, which extends from the Massachusetts/New Hampshire state border south to Manomet Point, Plymouth, Massachusetts, extending 200 nautical miles (370 km) off shore. Captain Gelzer was commissioned as a Coast Guard officer in 1991. She answered questions about her career by e-mail.

Q: Why did you join the Coast Guard?

A: After graduating from college, I worked as a newspaper reporter for two years, but I wanted to find a more service-oriented job. I thought about the police or fire department, but I was ultimately drawn to the Coast Guard's humanitarian and environmental response mission. I wanted to save lives, protect the environment, and go after drug traffickers at sea; the Coast Guard afforded me all those opportunities.

Q: Describe the role of sector commander and how you got the job?

A: Coast Guard sectors are multi-missioned units responsible for all 11 Coast Guard missions: marine safety, marine environmental protection, search and rescue, aids to navigation, ice breaking, living marine fisheries, drug interdiction, defense operations, ports and waterways coastal security, alien migrant interdiction, and other law enforcement. There are only thirty-five sectors positioned in major US ports and territories, so there is a lot of competition to be selected as a sector commander. Being a sector commander carries a tremendous amount of responsibility. To be eligible, you need to be a senior Coast Guard officer at the Captain/O-6 level with twenty-two years or more of service ideally specializing in shore-based operations. I was selected as sector commander for the Port of Boston because of my experience and record of performance working at marine safety offices, sectors, and a marine safety unit, of which I held command previously. A sector commander has the broadest regulatory and legal authority of all

71

Coast Guard operational commanders, and wears five different hats of authority, including: Captain of the Port (COTP), Search and Rescue Mission Coordinator (SMC), Officer in Charge Marine Inspection (OCMI), Federal on Scene Coordinator (FOSC), and Federal Maritime Security Coordinator (FMSC). As sector commander, I lead 400 active duty and 1,200 reserve, civilian, and auxiliary personnel; I also oversee five small boat stations, two patrol boats, one icebreaking cutter, and an Aids to Navigation Team.

Q: How did you train for this career?

A: The Coast Guard has provided me continual training opportunities throughout my career. My training began with Officer Candidate School, a seventeen-week indoctrination program through which I earned my commission as an ensign. Officers can also attend the Coast Guard Academy to receive a commission while earning a college degree. Enlisted members attend an eight-week boot camp as their initial training. Officers and enlisted continue training throughout their careers. As a mid-grade officer (lieutenant), the Coast Guard sent me full time with pay to earn a Master of Science in Environmental Management, and then later as a senior officer (Commander/O-5) for a Master of Arts in National Security and Strategic Studies at the Naval War College. Beyond formal education, officers and enlisted receive numerous on-the-job field and classroom training opportunities throughout a career.

Q: Can you describe your typical workday?

A: No day as a sector commander is the same [as any other]. That is one of the benefits of being in the Coast Guard, there is no typical day. Like I said before, we are multi-missioned. As the sector commander, my day begins with a morning briefing in the 24/7 Command Center to review all current and future operations for the coming day. On any given day, my teams are responding to search-and-rescue cases and oil spills, they are conducting law enforcement boardings on recreational boats and large commercial ships at sea, they are inspecting commercial ships and waterfront facilities to ensure safety and security, they are positioning aids to navigation to mark the channels or repairing a light house, and they are investigating ship accidents to identify unsafe practices and prevent recurrences. All of these operations and more are conducted to ensure the safety and security of the port, balanced with the movement of important cargo, including fuel, building materials, and containerized cargo. Throughout the day and after hours, I am asked to approve operations and set priorities on how we use our people and equipment. I partner closely with numerous port stakeholders including law enforcement and public safety agencies, and work with the maritime industry to ensure commercial operations are safe and secure.

Q: What do you like most and least about your job?

A: My favorite part of the job is leading the sector in operations that save lives and protect the environment. The best experience in the world is when my teams find a mariner in trouble at sea and bring them home safely. I also get satisfaction from partnering with port stakeholders to combine our collective efforts and resources to solve complex problems for the well-being of the port and public. The hardest days involve cases of loss of life at sea, and having to notify a mariner's family of bad news. These notifications are extremely important and require empathy, professionalism, and responsiveness to give the family comfort and closure.

Q: What personal qualities do you find most valuable for this type of work?

A: Strong work ethic and character, positive attitude, loyalty, empathy, and selflessness with a good sense of humor; must also be a strong communicator, a constant learner, and a team player who does not care who gets the credit as long as the job is done well. The Coast Guard's core values of honor, respect, and devotion to duty are at the core of every Coast Guard member and are a necessity for the work that we do daily.

Q: What is one thing that people might not know about this career?

A: The Coast Guard is the fifth branch of the armed services and has fought in every major conflict in US history, including most recently, the Iraq war. However, the primary focus of Coast Guard missions is to protect people on the sea, protect the US against threats delivered from the sea, and protect the sea itself. The Coast Guard is far smaller than the other military branches—approximately 40,000 active duty personnel—but it punches well above its weight class.

Q: What advice do you have for students who might be interested in this career?

A: Do your homework and get as much information as you can about the missions of the Coast Guard, its organization and career paths for officers and enlisted so you can make the best possible decisions at the beginning of your career. We are stationed around the country and US territories on our nation's ports and waterways, so you must like the ocean. Talk to a Coast Guard member and/or visit a Coast Guard unit to observe firsthand what we do.

Find Out More

Bureau of Labor Statistics: Occupational Outlook Handbook: Military
www.bls.gov/ooh/military/military-careers.htm
This website offers extensive information about careers and jobs in all branches of military service, including the Coast Guard. Learn about the work environment, job outlook, and what specific service members do.

Today's Military
http://todaysmilitary.com
Maintained by the Department of Defense, the goal of this website is to present an accurate picture of life in all the branches of the military. Visitors can learn about jobs, enlisted and officer careers, pay, training, and much more.

US Coast Guard
www.uscg.mil
The Department of Homeland Security's official Coast Guard website offers recent articles and stories of general interest, a description of the Coast Guard's organization, a detailed explanation of the Coast Guard's missions, and an overview of Coast Guard careers.

US Coast Guard Academy
www.uscga.edu
Find out about applying to and attending the Coast Guard Academy. Take a virtual tour of the campus, learn about the experience on the Coast Guard training vessel *The Eagle*, read about life as a cadet, and explore the admissions process.

US Coast Guard/Coast Guard Reserve
www.gocoastguard.com
The official website of the Coast Guard describes its mission, careers, benefits, and how to find out more about joining the service.

US Coast Guard Official Facebook Page
www.facebook.com/UScoastguard
Managed by the Coast Guard, this Facebook page provides a forum for discussing the Coast Guard's work.

Other Jobs in the Coast Guard

Accounting Officer
Air Station Commander
Aviation Maintenance
   Technician
Avionics Electrical Technician
Clinical and Rehabilitation
   Therapist
Communications Officer
Dental Officer
Deputy Sector Commander
District Commander
Diver
Electrician's Mate
Engineer
Environmental Health Officer
Food Service Specialist
Gunner's Mate

Health Services Officer
Information Systems Technician
Intelligence Officer
Intelligence Specialist
Lawyer
Machinery Technician
Maritime Enforcement
   Specialist
Musician
Nurse
Pharmacist
Physician
Public Affairs Specialist
Ship Officer
Storekeeper
Training Officer
Yeoman

Index

About the Author

Toney Allman holds degrees from Ohio State University and the University of Hawaii. She currently lives in Virginia, where she enjoys a rural lifestyle as well as researching and writing about a variety of topics for students.